At Sea

Ann Kramer

W
FRANKLIN WATTS
LONDON•SYDNEY

IN ASSOCIATION WITH

IMPERIAL WAR
MUSEUM

First published in 2010 by Franklin Watts

Copyright © 2010 Franklin Watts

Franklin Watts
338 Euston Road
London NW1 3BH

Franklin Watts Australia
Level 17/207 Kent Street
Sydney, NSW 2000

A CIP catalogue record for this book is available
from the British Library.

Dewey number: 940.5'45'0922

ISBN 978 0 7496 8819 6

Printed in China

Franklin Watts is a division of Hachette Children's Books,
an Hachette UK company.

www.hachette.co.uk

Editor: Sarah Ridley
Design: Billin Design Solutions
Editor in Chief: John C. Miles
Art director: Jonathan Hair

With many thanks to Nick Hewitt and the staff at the Imperial
War Museum's Document, Sound and Photograph Archives.

Picture credits:

Contents

At sea

In September 1939, Britain and France declared war on Nazi Germany, which had invaded Poland. The war lasted six years and involved nearly every country in the world. Much fighting took place at sea.

In 1939, Britain's Royal Navy was the strongest in the world. Its warships included battleships, submarines, destroyers and aircraft carriers. The main naval base was at Scapa Flow, in Orkney, but the navy had bases elsewhere in the United Kingdom as well as in the Mediterranean and the Far East. Britain also had the largest merchant navy in the world.

> **"**The day war was declared, the Admiral called us together in the wardroom and gave us champagne and gave us a toast — 'Damnation to Hitler'.**"**
>
> *Dick Caldwell, Surgeon-Lieutenant, Royal Navy*

'Mighty Hood'

Seen between two massive guns, HMS Hood *was the Royal Navy's pride and joy. In 1941, the German warship* Bismarck *sank the* Hood *during a sea battle in the Denmark Straits.*

Leabharlanna Poiblí Chathair Bhaile Átha Cliath
Dublin City Public Libraries

War at sea

British sailors saw action throughout the world, braving the elements from the Atlantic to the Mediterranean and into icy Arctic waters. They defended Britain's coastal waters, protected merchant shipping and battled with enemy warships and submarines. The navy carried land troops into battle, evacuated Allied forces, and launched aircraft from huge carriers. War at sea was immensely dangerous. Thousands on both sides lost their lives.

Sea power

Nations had fought battles at sea for hundreds of years but sea power during the Second World War was deadlier and more complicated than ever. Warships bristled with huge guns. Submarines were loaded with torpedoes and underwater mines were a hidden danger. But as war continued the nature of sea power changed. New and swifter ships were built. There were developments such as radar, which could track enemy vessels accurately, and aircraft played a greater role.

Standing to attention

The crew of HMS Rodney *stand ready for inspection next to the battleship's 16 inch (406 mm) gun turrets. HMS* Rodney *carried a crew of more than 1,000 men.*

> **"**I had no break from the time I finished my School Certificate and starting work in the dockyard... I was working on torpedoes... and... [churning]... out the goods for the navy... there was no time for things other than work...**"**

John Starling, dockyard apprentice, Portsmouth

Into action

For the first few months after war was declared there was little fighting on land. But war at sea began immediately. Sailors of all ranks sometimes found themselves under fire within hours.

In 1939, several thousand men and women were already serving in the navy. Some had served during the First World War (1914-18). When war began, reserves were called up and compulsory service was introduced for men and women over the age of 18. Life in the navy was hard but it was a respected service and a popular choice. Recruits, some as young as 15, volunteered to join. After training, personnel remained on shore or went to sea, serving in a huge variety of posts, such as officers, seamen, gunners and doctors.

Keeping a watch

Standing in the crow's nest, a sailor watches for enemy ships approaching Plymouth harbour. The navy laid nets reinforced with explosives across harbour entrances so enemy ships could not enter without being blown up.

Coastal defence

Invasion was a real fear. Harbour defences were set up and naval personnel watched for enemy warships. Minesweepers also patrolled the coasts: in 1939, a German magnetic mine was uncovered on the Essex coast. In October 1939, a German submarine managed to penetrate Scapa Flow and torpedo the battleship *Royal Oak*, which sank with the loss of 800 men.

> **"**I saw my first real action on 14 September. We were exercising with *Ark Royal* and three destroyers... there were two terrific explosions — we went to action stations immediately... A German U-boat had fired two torpedoes at *Ark Royal*... We... dropped... depth charges and up she came. It was U-39...**"**
>
> *Vernon Coles, Stoker 2nd Class, HMS* Faulknor

On fire, 1939

*German 'pocket battleship'
Graf Spee goes up in flames.
Three British cruisers — Exeter,
Ajax and Achilles — had
trapped the vessel in
Montevideo, Uruguay. The
crew believed more British
warships were on their way,
so they blew the ship up rather
than losing her to the enemy.*

Into action

Out at sea the navy
defended British shipping and blockaded German ports,
attempting to cut off their supplies. Losses were heavy as
German U-boats (submarines) and warships attacked British
warships. The German battleship *Graf Spee* sank nine British
merchant ships until, in December 1939, British cruisers
trapped her in a South American port.

**"... There was I, a young chap of
twenty, actually dropping things to
kill people..."**

John Roxburgh, Sub-Lieutenant, HMS Walpole

Advice

*Three 16-year-old sailors on HMS
King George V listen to advice
from 48-year-old Petty Officer
Jenman, who had already served in
the navy for 20 years.*

Evacuating Dunkirk

In May 1940, German forces overran Holland and Belgium, and invaded France. Thousands of British and French soldiers were trapped on the coast of northern France. The navy was ordered to rescue them.

Rescue mission

British troops board HMS Vanquisher at Dunkirk. Her crew made seven trips across the Channel, rescuing more than 2,200 soldiers.

A lot of work went into organising the rescue mission. Sailors on leave were told to report for duty — messages were flashed across cinema screens — and reservists were called up. Appeals also went out for civilian sailors.

A motley fleet

Within days a fleet of about 850 large and small ships was assembled. It included naval destroyers but also hundreds of civilian craft: fishing boats, pleasure cruisers, ferries, barges and yachts.

Setting out

Ships set out on 26 May. The Channel was calm and as sailors approached Dunkirk in France, they saw long lines of soldiers on the beaches. Larger warships could only take on soldiers at high tide from the jetty, so smaller boats went in close to the beach and ferried soldiers out to larger ships waiting offshore, making one trip after another.

Wreckage

A sunken trawler lies alongside a naval destroyer at Dunkirk. The approach to the beaches was littered with the wreckage of ships hit by German bombers.

"... we crossed the Channel under heavy attack by bombers but we landed on the jetty at Dunkirk... for the first 48 hours I was never off my feet...**"**

Lieutenant Bruce Junor

Exhausting

Sailors — naval and civilian — worked non-stop to evacuate the soldiers, often under intense enemy fire. Many ships were sunk or wrecked. As ships filled with soldiers, their crews made the return journey to Britain. Once there, soldiers disembarked and crews returned to France, often crossing at night. Sailors were exhausted but within 10 days they had evacuated more than 338,000 Allied troops.

"... Most of them [soldiers] were stretcher cases and walking wounded... We cleared the mess decks to make room... There were two or three hundred on board, plus about 60 of us crew...**"**

Dick Coppeard, Ordinary Seaman

Sinking queen, 1940

The SS Mona's Queen was an Isle of Man ferry. Its crew took part in the evacuation. They hit a mine and sank. HMS Vanquisher rescued survivors.

Battle of the Atlantic

German and British navies fought each other in the grey, hostile waters of the Atlantic Ocean throughout the war. The Battle of the Atlantic was the longest continuous battle of the war.

Britain needed its merchant shipping to bring in essential supplies and keep trade flowing to pay for the war. But as Allied sailors braved the elements, the German navy attacked them using aircraft, surface raiders like the battleship *Bismarck* — and U-boats.

U-boats

Germany's navy was smaller than Britain's but its U-boats were lethal. Travelling silently under water, they struck without notice, surfacing at night. After the *Bismarck* was sunk in 1941, U-boats were the biggest threat to Allied shipping.

Allied losses

Engagements in the Atlantic stretched over hundreds of kilometres. Destroyer crews spent weeks at sea, constantly on the look out for the enemy. Conditions were awful; storms were common and waves could reach 10 metres high. The death toll was enormous.

> **"Our life consisted of going on watch, coming off watch and crawling into the hammock for a bit of relief from the pitching and rolling..."**
>
> *Donald Auffret, wireless operator, HMS Sweetbriar, escorting Atlantic convoys*

A hit, 1941

British crew watch as depth charges that they fired explode above a German U-boat. The Royal Navy developed increasingly effective ways of finding and destroying U-boats.

> *"... we saw the Bismarck ahead... the whole fleet sort of opened fire... I was a gun-layer on the four-inch gun... We'd fired 257 eight-inch-shells (20-cm) at the Bismarck... we went in as close as we could and fired two (torpedoes)... eventually she sort of rolled over and went down..."*
>
> Herbert Gollop, Able Seaman, HMS Dorsetshire

In 1941, U-boats sank more than 1,200 Allied ships. In 1942, they sank more than 1,600.

Gaining the upper hand

Gradually the situation changed. Britain set up naval bases in Iceland, and Allied navies helped the Royal Navy to escort merchant shipping. Longer-range aircraft provided greater air support. A submarine detection system called ASDIC that pinpointed enemy submarines using sound waves was invaluable. And experts cracked the German naval code, which gave Britain valuable information about U-boats. By 1943, the Allies were winning the Battle of the Atlantic.

Long-range weapon

Aircraft such as this Consolidated Liberator of 220 Squadron Royal Air Force based at Lagens, Azores, provided vital air support during the Battle of the Atlantic.

Pack hunters

A German U-boat commander tracks a British ship through his periscope. Later in the war, U-boats hunted in packs, like wolves. Their crews spent weeks at sea.

Merchant navy

Britain's merchant navy was the largest in the world. Its ships ranged from great ocean liners through to oil tankers and coastal tugs. It carried essential supplies — food, fuel, troops and equipment — wherever they were needed.

A busy dock

Dockers shift goods from river barges to merchant ships for transport. During the war, the merchant navy worked hard to make sure much-needed goods reached Britain.

Unlike the Royal Navy, merchant seamen were civilians. Some were from Britain but seamen from India, Africa, Canada and other parts of the Commonwealth also served in the British merchant navy. There were also merchant ships and seamen from Allied and neutral powers, including Norway, Sweden and Greece.

Immediate attack

Attacks on merchant shipping started on the first day of war. On 3 September 1939, just a few hours after war was declared, a torpedo from a German U-boat hit the British passenger liner *Athenia*. More than 100 people lost their lives.

Sinking

Hit by a torpedo, this merchant ship sinks into Atlantic waves, stern first. In 1942, U-boats sank 5.4 million tonnes of Allied merchant shipping.

"... the bombing attacks started again... a large plane flew right over us... dropped a salvo of six bombs... The *Ohio* was lifted right out of the water... at approximately 18.30 a plane dropped a bomb directly on the fore part of the boat deck... the crew were blinded and choked by the powder from the asbestos lagging...**"**

Dudley Mason, captain of the oil tanker Ohio. *Despite damage, the tanker reached Malta harbour*

From then on merchant ships and their crew came under constant attack, particularly in the Atlantic but also in the Mediterranean and around the coast of Britain. U-boats, German bombers and surface vessels all preyed on Allied merchant shipping.

A dangerous life

Merchant seamen faced the same dangers as men in the armed forces but their ships were peacetime vessels. Some were armed, but none were fully equipped to counteract enemy attacks. By the end of the war, at least 34,000 merchant seamen had lost their lives, more than 3,000 of them boys under the age of 18.

Lucky man

Merchant seaman Albert Prince served as a steward in the merchant navy. He was lucky to survive. Four separate ships he served on were hit: one by a bomb, one by a mine, and two by torpedoes.

13

Convoy

Ploughing through mountainous waves, great convoys of merchant shipping travelled across the North Atlantic. Naval warships provided armed escort and protection.

It was easy for U-boats to pick off single ships so by 1941 merchant shipping, carrying fuel, troops, or military equipment, travelled in convoy with warship escorts for safety. Some convoys were quite small; others, particularly those that crossed the Atlantic or sailed around the British coast, included 50 or more ships.

Escort vessels

The British navy, together with the American and Canadian navies, had the job of protecting the convoys. Ideally, destroyers travelled in front and to the rear of convoys. Smaller ships, such as corvettes or frigates, travelled at the sides, circling slow-moving merchant shipping or edging them back into line. Escort vessels carried guns and depth charges. They also carried big crews, including officers, gunners, radio

Convoy, 1943

Stretching as far as the eye can see, a British convoy makes its way across the Atlantic. Allied aircraft sometimes provided air cover as well.

Re-fuelling, 1942

Buffeted by high seas, a British destroyer re-fuels from a cruiser alongside in the middle of the North Atlantic. It was dangerous work re-fuelling in these conditions.

operators, stokers, sick bay attendants and cooks. Those on watch kept a constant look out for enemy submarines, aircraft and mines.

Long journeys

Convoys crossed the Atlantic regularly. It was a slow business and ships often became separated. Sailors were at sea for weeks, often in dreadful weather. Many seamen became exhausted and even the most experienced sailors could suffer from seasickness. Convoys also travelled the Mediterranean carrying supplies to Malta. From 1941, Arctic convoys began taking supplies from Britain to the Soviet Union.

Stormy seas

Atlantic waves crash over HMS Inglefield, *which is protecting merchant ships that are carrying vital food supplies and war equipment.*

Frozen signals, 1941

A naval signalman continues signalling to the convoy while ice forms on his projector. One seaman said that it was so cold on the Arctic convoys that the hairs in his nostrils froze.

“I was 15 when I joined the navy... I was on the Russian convoys to Murmansk... Our role was ahead of the convoy... to shelter it or protect it... The conditions... were very cold and there were constant alarms for aircraft and surface vessels... the guns would get iced up and you had to chip it off...”

Joseph Stagno, boy seaman, HMS Belfast

Abandoning ship

Torpedoes, bombs and mines took a deadly toll on ships and crews of both sides during the war. If a ship sank, the chances of survival were slight.

Shell blasts wrecked ships and caused dreadful casualties. Losses were high. In May 1941 the German battleship *Bismarck* attacked and sank HMS *Hood*. More than 1,400 officers and men died in the explosion or in the sea. Only three survived. Days later the Royal Navy sank the *Bismarck*. Only 115 men survived from a crew of 2,200.

Abandoning ship

Damaged vessels could sink within minutes. Seamen were forced to abandon ship. Some died when the ship sucked them down. Others floundered in waves thick with oil. Nearby vessels picked up survivors but sometimes were forced to leave men in the water because they were vulnerable to attack when stopped. In Arctic waters a man might only survive for four minutes.

Scrambling to safety, 1943

Sailors scramble up nets from an inflatable raft onto a rescue ship. They are practising for the real thing. Small rescue ships sometimes travelled with Atlantic convoys; their job was to rescue survivors from the water.

66 Then the order came from the bridge to abandon ship... I floated on a chunk of wood until I was picked up. A lot of the people that were brought on board, with oil fuel and shock, had died. They were stacking the bodies like you would firewood... 99

John Gaynor, Petty Officer, HMS Prince of Wales

Direct hit

Covered in oil, an officer of HMS Manchester emerges from below deck after a torpedo has hit the ship. Other crewmen are still trapped below.

Exposure

Most seamen wore inflatable jackets or belts to keep them afloat. Some survivors scrambled into circular shaped inflatable rafts. These contained flares, water bottles and first-aid kits but there was no protection from the elements. Some men floated for hours or days. Many died from exposure.

Treatment

Most larger warships carried doctors, who treated wounded in sick bays until they could be taken ashore. During battles, or evacuations, they worked around the clock. The navy also had a number of fully equipped hospital ships.

Safe, 1942

Survivors from the British frigate HMS Naid, which was torpedoed by a German U-boat in the Mediterranean, smile happily for the camera.

> **"**One of the hits went through the bridge and killed everyone there except the captain, the chief yeoman and the navigator — who was very seriously wounded...**"**
>
> Colin McMullen, Gunnery Officer, HMS Prince of Wales

Wrens

The navy was seen as a man's world but women served as well. Thousands of women joined the Women's Royal Naval Service (WRNS). They were known as Wrens.

Many young women over the age of 18 wanted to join the navy, which was seen as a desirable service. Some recruits came from privileged backgrounds and already knew how to sail. But getting into the WRNS was not easy and there was a waiting list. New recruits went through two weeks' training, learning naval procedures, signalling and how to drill.

Signalling
Dressed in full uniform, a Wren uses signal flags to send a message. Signallers used semaphore during the war as well as Morse and radar.

Duties

At first Wrens were used only as typists, clerks and cooks but their duties soon expanded. Wrens worked as signallers, engineers, electricians, photographers and radio operators in operations rooms. They also delivered dispatches, driving motorcycles through the blackout.

Safe as rocks, 1944
Two Wren officers pore over charts in a naval operations room in Gibraltar. Their office is in a tunnel inside the rock, making it one of the safest air-raid shelters in the world.

> "My ambition was to join the WRNS... but it took me a whole year... They always had a waiting list and I was not privileged in any way, despite my father's high position in the Royal Navy... When I eventually joined... I chose Signals... an interesting department in the heart of what was happening..."
>
> *Patricia Mountbatten, Countess Mountbatten of Burma, London*

Going to sea

Wrens were mainly based on shore. The navy did not want mixed crews and warships were too crowded to provide separate quarters for men and women. However, Wrens worked on harbour craft and served as signallers on Atlantic liners. From 1941, Wrens were posted abroad.

No fighting

Women in the navy were paid less than men and, as with other service women, were not allowed to fight or go into combat. They did not serve in gun crews but they did work with torpedoes, as mechanics and maintenance workers.

Wrens everywhere

Indian, West Indian and other Commonwealth women joined the WRNS. In 1944 the Women's Royal Indian Naval Service was formed.

Moving torpedoes, 1943

Four Wrens wheel a torpedo ready to be loaded onto a submarine. From 1942, Wrens worked as electricians in the torpedo branch of the navy. They were not allowed to fire torpedoes or guns.

Mines and minesweepers

Mines were a serious threat to ships. Minesweepers and their crews worked to clear them.

Thousands of mines were laid during the war. They included contact mines, which were moored to the bottom of the sea with a weighted cable. The mine had horns: if a ship's hull came into contact with one of the horns, the firing mechanism was activated. Others included magnetic mines, which were detonated by the magnetic field of a ship's hull, and acoustic mines that were set off by the sound of a ship.

Gently does it

Sailors in a small rowing boat shackle a floating mine to a towing wire so it can be made safe at Singapore.

Laying mines

The British used coastal ships, warships and destroyers to lay mines. They also used submarines. Specialist divers or frogmen sometimes laid mines in enemy harbours, using a submarine to do so. The Luftwaffe, RAF and US Air Force dropped thousands of sea mines, attached to parachutes.

> **"**... all we had to do was drop these mines between ship [German battleship *Tirpitz*] and shore and they would go down and do their stuff... [but]... the drop was not accurate... We lost about half the aircraft that were on the raid...**"**
>
> *Donald Bennett, Wing Commander 10 Squadron RAF, 1943*

Minesweeping

The navy used various ships to clear mines. They included converted paddle steamers and fishing boats through to specially built vessels. Ships worked singly or in flotillas. To clear normal moored mines, ships literally 'swept' the mines from the sea floor by dragging a cable behind them. Cutters on the ship's cable sliced through the mine cables, and freed mines floated to the surface. Marksmen then shot the floating mines to blow them up. About 57,000 sailors, including fishermen, worked on board minesweepers during the war.

Home to port

This photo shows a fishing trawler, HMT Fyldea, *having been converted to minesweeping duties, underway near the entrance to Dover harbour.*

Blown up

The crew of the minesweeper HMS Hebe *cleared mines in the Channel and the Mediterranean. In 1943, mines laid by a U-boat blew up the* Hebe, *which sank with the loss of 38 men.*

> "... we scraped along the sea-bed... we were all sweating, especially Magennis in his diving gear... [he] could hardly squeeze himself out of the hatch... we had to wait while he laid the mines... he'd had to cut away thick weed and scrape away... barnacles before the magnets on the mine would stick to the hull..."
>
> *Ian Fraser, pilot of a Royal Navy midget submarine laying mines in Singapore*

Communications

The navy needed to communicate with ships in oceans across the world. Ships had to communicate with each other, and they needed to track enemy craft. Skilled personnel passed messages, plotted courses and detected enemy submarines and warships.

Traditionally the navy used semaphore or signalling flags as a secure way to send messages between ships; these were still used during the war. Signallers had to be well trained to send messages quickly and accurately. In poor weather or when signalling to a convoy whose ships stretched out for kilometres, signallers used lamps to send messages in Morse code.

Radio and wireless

Wireless operators also used radiotelephony, or voice radio, for ship-to-ship or ship-to-shore communication. Wireless operators wearing headphones sat at radio sets on shore or at sea, receiving messages that had to be passed on very quickly. Wireless operators also sent messages in Morse code.

Signaller, 1942

A Royal Navy signaller using an Aldis lamp on board HMS Shropshire. *He opens and closes a shutter on the lamp to send messages in Morse code.*

Radar

A radar operator sits in his action station in a British convoy escort. Blips on his screen may indicate enemy warships or aircraft. He passes the information to the bridge using a voice pipe.

Detection

The Royal Navy used two main detection systems during the war. ASDIC, or sonar, transmitted sound waves that bounced off a submerged object, such as a submarine, and revealed its location to the operator through headphones. Radar detected surface ships and aircraft by transmitting radio waves that also bounced off the object and back to the ship. Objects appeared as small 'blips' of light on a screen. Radar operators interpreted these signals and passed information to the captain on the bridge.

Tracking convoys, 1941

Two officers track the course of a convoy in the North Atlantic, moving coded markers around a huge wall map. Operators worked day and night to check the progress of convoys. Built of steel and concrete, the operations room was underground in Liverpool.

"During these attacks we were constantly receiving orders by wireless to make 45 degree emergency turns... These orders were also transmitted over the radio telephone and the wireless orders were always several seconds behind... causing misunderstanding and confusion...**"**

Dudley Mason, captain of the oil tanker Ohio, *describing attacks off Malta, 1942*

Submarines

British submarines prowled the seas from Norway to the Mediterranean and the Far East. Loaded with torpedoes, they targeted enemy ships and penetrated enemy ports.

By 1944 some 9,000 sailors, known as submariners, were serving in submarines. They had to be fit and do weeks of intensive training. It was a dangerous job. If a submarine was lost, its crew usually went with it.

Thunderbolt

HMS/M Thunderbolt floats in a harbour after a patrol. British submarines patrolled singly, or in pairs, unlike German U-boats, which hunted in packs later in the war.

Crowded

Submarines carried a large crew of officers and men. Accommodation, engines and torpedoes were all squashed into the hull. The air became hot and stuffy and everything smelled of diesel. Meals could not be cooked while submerged, so submariners ate cold food and rested to save oxygen.

To avoid enemy attacks, submarines often submerged during the day and used their electric motors. They surfaced at night, running on diesel

Up periscope

A submarine officer peers through the periscope. A periscope could only be used in shallow water and had to be used sparingly. Enemy aircraft could spot periscopes, and so could lookouts on enemy ships.

> **"**...My plan... was to dive down deep... pass under the torpedo nets... lay the charges, then escape under the nets... we were now about 30 yards from the *Tirpitz*'s port beam... we slid underneath and dropped one charge forward... and aft... while we were struggling to get free... the explosion went up... [it] shook us free but... damaged X7...**"**
>
> *Godfrey Place, Lieutenant, X-craft submariner, Royal Navy, describing the attack by midget submarines on German battleship* Tirpitz *in a Norwegian harbour, 1943*

engines to charge their batteries. Men took turns on watch. There were not enough bunks for everyone, so as one man went on watch, another took his bunk.

Attacking and diving

Submarines were attacking machines. They travelled faster on the surface and often attacked on the surface, firing torpedoes through tubes. The captain directed the firing. From 1942 the navy used 'midget' submarines, with a crew of only four, which slid into shallow harbour waters to attack ships.

If a submarine spotted an enemy aircraft or warship, a siren sounded and the submarine 'crash' dived, dropping just over 18 metres (60 feet) within a minute. Tension mounted as the crew waited in case they were hit by an enemy's depth charge.

Cramped quarters

Submariners relax in the mess, which is also the torpedo storage compartment. Accommodation on board a submarine was very cramped.

Into the air

As well as ships, the navy also operated aircraft. Unlike the land-based RAF, the navy's aircraft were often based at sea, taking off from huge, armoured vessels called aircraft carriers.

Aircraft carriers became increasingly important as war continued. They launched aircraft that could travel quickly to attack targets far out at sea. They provided air support for convoys, and launched aircraft from the sea to hit land targets.

Bases at sea

The Royal Navy had seven aircraft carriers in 1939 but built more. Some were converted from other ships; others were custom made. The largest carried up to 60 aircraft, stored in steel reinforced hangars below decks. Lifts brought the aircraft from the hangars to the flight deck. Carriers, like other warships, carried a big crew of officers and men, but also pilots, navigators, armourers and aircraft maintenance staff.

Take off, 1942

A Fairey Albacore, fitted with a torpedo, takes off from the flight deck of aircraft carrier HMS Victorious. Once in the air, pilots and navigators had the difficult job of finding their target over miles of sea with no landmarks.

> **“**... It was dark, there were no lights and the carrier was moving the whole time... One would only have to be blown ten miles off course by an adverse wind and one would never find the carrier. As it was, my pilot made a perfect landing.**”**
>
> David Goodwin, Lieutenant, 824 Squadron, on returning to HMS Illustrious *from a raid on Taranto, Italy, 1940*

Skilled techniques

Taking off from and landing on an aircraft carrier was a skilled operation. For take off, the ship turned into the wind. Pilots started their run from the stern and, at a flag signal from the flight deck officer, took off over the bows. On large carriers, aircraft could launch every 15 seconds.

Deck landings were even more difficult. A batsman guided the pilot in. As he landed, the pilot applied his brakes, the aircraft snagged on an arrestor wire to slow it down, the pilot brought the flaps up, and took the brakes off. Crashes were common, and many pilots died.

Wheeling a bomb, 1944

Armourers wheel a 500 lb bomb along the flight deck of HMS Formidable, *a huge aircraft carrier. Planes from this carrier attacked the German warship* Tirpitz *in Norway.*

Deck landing

A batsman guides a Fairey Swordfish in for a deck landing. Putting a plane down on a moving carrier was a tricky manoeuvre. There were many accidents.

D-Day landings

On 6 June 1944, more than 6,500 landing craft and ships, laden with soldiers, artillery and tanks arrived on the coast of Normandy, France. It was the largest seaborne invasion in history. All three armed services took part. The navy took a key role.

The Royal Navy had taken troops into land battles earlier in the war. Americans too used amphibious warfare in the Pacific. But the Normandy landings — known as D-Day — were the largest and most complex. More than 95,000 naval and merchant navy personnel landed over 130,000 troops in just one day.

Careful planning

The British and Americans worked together to plan the invasion of France. Sailors underwent special training and everything had to be done in secret. Tides and weather also had to be right.

Ready to go

A fleet of landing craft lie alongside the quay at Southampton, ready and waiting to cross the English Channel to Normandy.

The invasion

On the night of 5 June, a massive armada set out from various British ports. It included barges, warships and landing ships, which carried British, American and Canadian troops, tanks, equipment and special landing craft. A storm had forced a 24-hour delay. Soldiers were seasick and waves broke over the bows.

The landings

Minesweepers had been at work since 2 am so when the navy arrived off the French coast, they sailed down narrow channels free of mines. Warships and RAF planes bombarded the coast. Soldiers and equipment transferred to special landing and assault craft, which took them onto the beaches. From there, Allied forces began the liberation of occupied Europe. Less than a year later the war in Europe was over.

Landing tanks, 1944

Specially designed landing craft offloaded tanks onto the beaches at Normandy. The craft had specially designed bow doors, which opened to allow tanks and other equipment to roll onto the beaches.

Mulberries

Tugs towed huge concrete structures called caissons across the Channel. They were assembled on the Normandy coast to make artificial harbours, known as Mulberry Harbours.

Glossary

Amphibious warfare War that takes place on both land and water.

Bridge Platform or room on a ship where the captain controls the course of the ship.

Convoy A group of ships travelling together, with an escort to protect them.

Corvette An armed escort vessel, smaller than a destroyer.

Depth charge A bomb that explodes underwater, used to attack submarines.

Drill, drilling Training in military exercises.

First World War (1914-18) Also called the 'Great War' or World War I. Fought between the Entente, which included Britain, France, Italy, Russia and the USA, and the Central Powers, which included Germany, Austria-Hungary and Turkey.

Flotilla A small group of ships moving together.

Luftwaffe German air force in the Second World War.

Merchant navy Non-military navy used for commercial and trading purposes, moving goods and equipment around the world.

Morse code A system for sending messages in which letters of the alphabet are represented by short and long light or sound signals.

Nazi Short for National Socialist. This was an extreme right-wing political party led by Adolf Hitler, the leader of Germany. It controlled Germany during the Second World War.

Occupied Europe European countries invaded and occupied by German forces during the Second World War. They included Belgium, northern France and the Netherlands.

Periscope A tube-like instrument on a submarine that allows crew members to see objects on the surface.

Radar Stands for Radio Direction and Ranging, originally called RDF (Radio Direction Finding). A system for locating objects, such as ships, with radio waves.

Royal Navy British armed naval service.

Second World War (1939-45) Also known as World War II. Fought between the Axis Powers, which included Germany, Italy and Japan, and the Allies, which included Britain and its Empire, France, Russia and the USA.

Semaphore A system for sending messages using hand-held flags that represent letters of the alphabet.

U-boat Stands for *Unterseeboot* (German for undersea boat) — a German military submarine.

Further information
Books

My Second World War, Daniel James, Franklin Watts in association with the Imperial War Museum, 2008

Posters and Propaganda in Wartime, Daniel James and Ruth Thomson, Franklin Watts in association with the Imperial War Museum, 2007

World War Two: The Home Front, Ann Kramer, Franklin Watts, 2006

Growing Up in World War Two, Catherine Burch, Franklin Watts, 2009

The Second World War, Dennis Hamley, Franklin Watts, 2007

War Machines: Ships, Simon Adams, Franklin Watts in association with the Imperial War Museum, 2007

Some useful websites

http://london.iwm.org.uk/upload/package/8/atlantic/index.htm
Imperial War Museum website about the Battle of the Atlantic.

http://www.bbc.co.uk/ww2peopleswar/categories/c1184/
BBC website where you can read people's own stories of serving in the Royal Navy during the Second World War.

http://www.bbc.co.uk/ww2peopleswar/categories/c1174/
BBC website where you can read what it was like to serve in the merchant navy.

http://www.liverpoolmuseums.org.uk/.../themerchantnavy.aspx
The story of Britain's wartime merchant navy on the website of the Merseyside Maritime Museum in Liverpool.

Note to parents and teachers:
Every effort has been made by the Publishers to ensure that the websites in this book are suitable for children, that they are of the highest educational value, and that they contain no inappropriate or offensive material. However, because of the nature of the Internet, it is impossible to guarantee that the contents of these sites will not be altered. We strongly advise that Internet access is supervised by a responsible adult.

Index